Smithsonian

LITTLE EXPLORER

BUZZING
BEES

Melissa Higgins

raintree
a Capstone company — publishers for children

Raintree is an imprint of Capstone Global Library Limited, a company incorporated in England and Wales having its registered office at 264 Banbury Road, Oxford, OX2 7DY – Registered company number: 6695582

www.raintree.co.uk
myorders@raintree.co.uk

Edited by Abby Colich
Designed by Kyle Grenz
Original illustrations © Capstone Global Library Limited 2020
Picture research by Kelly Garvin
Production by Tori Abraham
Originated by Capstone Global Library Ltd
Printed and bound in India

ISBN 978 1 4747 7057 6 (hardback)
ISBN 978 1 4747 7063 7 (paperback)
23 22 21 20 19
10 9 8 7 6 5 4 3 2 1

British Library Cataloguing in Publication Data
A full catalogue record for this book is available from the British Library.

Acknowledgements
We would like to thank the following for permission to reproduce photographs: Alamy: Genevieve Vallee, 27, Nature Collection, 23; Science Source/Scott Camazine, 17; Shutterstock: Anna Morgan, 1, Bachkova Natalia, 7, Daniel Prudeck, 2, 13, dwphotos, 7 (top inset), Ed Phillips, 21, Elliotte Rusty Harold, 29, Frank Reiser, 11 (top inset), Ian Grainger, 19, irin-k, 5, 25 (bottom inset), Jennifer Bosvert, 20, JSseng, 14, Marek Mierzejewski, 5, Moolkum, 22, NoPainNoGain, 8, PYP, 11, Rosafandi Rosli, 25, Sweet Crisis, 9, TB studio, cover

Our very special thanks to Gary Hevel, Public Information Officer (Emeritus), Entomology Department, at the Smithsonian National Museum of Natural History. Capstone would also like to thank Kealy Gordon, Product Development Manager, and the following at Smithsonian Enterprises: Ellen Nanney, Licensing Manager; Brigid Ferraro, Vice President, Education and Consumer Products; and Carol LeBlanc, Senior Vice President, Education and Consumer Products.

Contents

The buzz about bees

Have you ever seen bees buzzing around a flower? Bees are very important. They move pollen from one flower to another. This helps new plants to grow. Without bees, Earth would have fewer plants.

About 25,000 species of bees live on Earth. Some bees are social. They live with other bees in a hive. Other bees are solitary. They live and work alone.

Parts of a bee

Bees are insects. Bees have two pairs of wings. They also have two antennae and six legs. Some bees have hairy legs and stomachs. The hair collects pollen. Bees have long tongues for getting nectar from flowers.

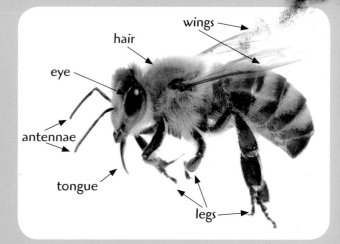

wings

hair

eye

antennae

tongue

legs

umble be_s

Number of species: 255
Found: worldwide in mild climates
Length: 1.5 to 2.5 centimetres (0.6 to 1 inches)

Bumble bees are good pollinators. Their heavy bodies and fast-beating wings shake pollen from flowers. A worker collects pollen on her fuzzy stomach. She carries it back to the hive. Young bees eat the pollen. Bumble bee hives are often on or under the ground. About 50 to 200 bumble bees share a hive.

DID YOU KNOW?

Most bees flap their wings up and down. Bumble bees move their wings back and forth.

Inside a hive

Three types of bees live in each hive. There are drones, workers and a queen. Workers are all female. They gather pollen and feed young bees. They also protect the hive. Drones are male. They mate with the queen. The queen lays eggs.

Carpenter bees

Number of species: more than 500
Found: worldwide except in the coldest climates
Length: 1.3 to 2.5 centimetres (0.5 to 1 inch)

Carpenter bees make nests in wood. A female drills small holes. She lays an egg in each hole. Then she places a ball of pollen near the egg. The egg hatches into a larva. The larva eats the pollen.

Life cycle of a bee

A bee begins life as an egg. The egg hatches into a larva. The larva eats and eats until it becomes a pupa. An adult emerges from the pupa.

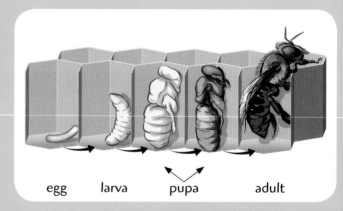

egg   larva   pupa   adult

Carpenter bees cut and tear into wood using mandibles. These are near the mouthparts on either side of the head.

cuckoo bees

Number: 5 to 15 per cent of all bees
Found: worldwide except in the coldest climates
Length: 0.6 to 1.3 centimetres (0.25 to 0.5 inches)

Cuckoo bees steal nests from other bees. Some cuckoo bees lay an egg in another bee's nest. The cuckoo bee's egg hatches first. It eats food meant for the other bee's larvae. Sometimes the cuckoo bee even eats the other larvae.

Other cuckoo bees invade another queen's hive. They kill the strongest workers. Then they show other workers their stingers. The frightened workers let the cuckoo bees stay. Some cuckoo bees kill the queen. Others live alongside her.

neon cuckoo bee

Bee stingers

Bees use their stingers to protect themselves. Most bees only sting when they feel threatened. Stingers contain venom. The venom slows down any predators. Only female bees have stingers. Some species don't have them at all.

Honey bees

Number of species: 7
Found: worldwide except Antarctica
Length: 0.8 to 1.8 centimetres (0.3 to 0.7 inches)

Honey bees are very social. A hive can have as many as 60,000 bees. Most of them are female workers. The workers do many jobs. Scouts look for food. Collectors gather pollen, nectar or water. House bees turn nectar into honey. They also feed the queen and take care of young bees. Guard bees protect the hive from predators.

The waggle dance

Scouts have an interesting way to tell collectors when they've found food. They do a dance in a figure of eight. Scientists call this the waggle dance. The longer a scout dances, the further away the food is.

Honey and beeswax

Only honey bees make honey that people eat. Worker bees chew nectar until it turns into honey. They store the honey inside a honeycomb. The honeycomb is made from wax. The wax started out as honey. Worker bees have glands that turn honey into wax.

Honey bees are important pollinators. They also make honey. Beekeepers build boxes that are perfect for hives. They place the boxes near crops that need to be pollinated. Then they collect the honey to eat or to sell. But honey bees are in danger. Diseases, mites and pesticides kill them. Scientists are working to help protect honey bees.

Killer bees

Number of species: 1
Found: South America, Central America and southern
      United States
Length: 0.8 to 1.8 centimetres (0.3 to 0.7 inches)

Killer bees are a strain of honey bee. Killer bees are very bold. They swarm faster than other bees. They travel in larger numbers too. Killer bees have the same amount of venom as honey bees. Victims can get thousands of stings. That many stings can kill an adult human.

DID YOU KNOW?

Killer bees have killed hundreds of humans.

Killer bees are also called Africanized honey bees.

Escaped bees

In 1957 a scientist in Brazil wanted to create bees that could make more honey. His bees escaped from the lab. They have moved north every year. Killer bees now live in the southern United States. The bees will keep moving until they reach places where it's too cold for them.

Leafcutter bees

Number of species: 4,100
Found: worldwide mostly in warm climates
Length: 1 to 2 centimetres (0.4 to 0.8 inches)

Leafcutter bees live alone. A female finds holes in logs, stems or the ground. She lines each hole with leaves. She lays an egg in each hole. Then she plugs the hole with more leaves. This helps to keep out predators. Her larvae eat pollen that she has left in the hole. Most young leafcutter bees stay in their nests over the winter. They grow into adults. They bite through the leaf plugs and come out in the spring.

DID YOU KNOW?

Mason bees are related to leafcutter bees. They use mud to make their nests instead of leaves.

Leafcutter bees cut round holes in leaves.

Bee eaters

Many animals eat bees. At least 24 types of birds eat them. Bears, weasels and mice do too. Lizards, frogs and toads might make a meal of adult bees or their young. Some insects and spiders eat bees as well.

Mining bees

Number of species: 1,500
Found: worldwide mostly in warm climates
Length: 0.8 to 1.8 centimetres (0.3 to 0.7 inches)

Mining bees dig holes in soil. A female makes a special liquid. Then she lines the hole with it. After the liquid dries, she rubs the dirt walls with her stomach. This polishes the soil. It becomes a sturdy and smooth nest for her young.

DID YOU KNOW?

Some mining bees like company. Tens of thousands might build their nests close together.

Mining bees often dig their nests near shrubs.
Each entrance is marked with a small mound of soil.

Oil collecting bees

Number of species: 26
Found: South Africa
Length: 0.5 cm to 1.3 centimetres (0.2 to 0.5 inches)

Oil-collecting bees only visit snapdragon flowers. These bees have very long legs. Their feet are covered with soft hairs. The hairs soak up oil from the flower. Females use the oil to line their nests. They also mix the oil with pollen. It makes a sort of bread. The bees feed it to their young.

snapdragon flowers

DID YOU KNOW?

Oil-collecting bees build their nests underground.

Vulture bees

Number of species: 3
Found: North and South America
Length: Up to 0.5 centimetres (0.2 inches)

Vulture bees do not feed on pollen or nectar. They eat the meat of dead animals. They also eat the eggs and larvae of wasps and toads. Vulture bees have sharp mouths. They work like teeth. Females mix meat with their saliva. It forms a goo. The goo is healthy for their young.

Bee or wasp?

Bees and wasps belong to the same group. Like most bees, female wasps have stingers with venom. But unlike most bees, wasps eat meat. Wasps have no hairs or pockets for collecting pollen. Their smooth, thin bodies are perfect for chasing prey.

bee

wasp

stingless bees

Number of species: 500
Found: worldwide mostly in tropical climates
Length: 0.5 centimetres (0.2 inches)

Stingless bees do have stingers.
But the stingers are very small.
They can't hurt anyone they
sting. They protect their hives
in other ways. Some stingless
bees use soldiers. These female
workers guard the entrance
to a hive. They use strong
mandibles to bite invaders.
A soldier will not let go of an
invader. The bee may even
hang on until it dies.

stingless bees in their nest

Sweat bees

Number of species: 4,300
Found: every continent except Antarctica
Length: 0.3 to 1.3 centimetres (0.1 to 0.5 inches)

Sweat bees are attracted to human sweat. Many people consider these bees pests and swat them away. Luckily, sweat bees don't often sting.

Some sweat bees are social. They live in a hive with a queen. But most are solitary. Each female builds her own nests. The nests are often underground. Some sweat bees are both social and solitary. Several females share a hive.

The bodies of some sweat bees are brightly coloured and shiny.

Becoming a queen

Queen bees give off a scent when they get old. This tells worker bees it's time for a new queen. Worker bees start feeding a special food to female larvae. These bees grow into queens. New queens fight to the death until only one remains.

Glossary

gland organ in the body that makes certain chemicals

larva insect at the stage of development between an egg and an adult

mandibles strong mouthparts used to chew

mate join together to produce young

mite creature that lives and feeds on some insects and animals

nectar sweet liquid that some insects collect from flowers and eat as food

pesticide poisonous chemical used to kill insects, rats and fungi that can damage plants

pollen powder that flowers make to help them create new seeds

predator animal that hunts other animals for food

prey animal that is hunted by another animal for food

social living in groups or packs

solitary living and hunting alone

species group of living things that can reproduce with one another

swarm gather or fly close together in a large group

venom poisonous liquid produced by some animals

Think about bees!

1. How many known species of bees are there in the world? Where do they live?

2. Killer bees look like honey bees. In what ways are they different? Use the text to help you with your answer.

3. In what ways are bees helpful?

Find out more

Books

Bees and Wasps: Secrets of Their Busy Colonies (Amazing Animal Colonies), Sara L. Latta (Raintree, 2019)

Bees and Wasps, James Maclaine (Usborne, 2013)

Insects and Spiders: Explore Nature with Fun Facts and Activities (Nature Explorers), DK (DK Children, 2019)

Websites

www.bbc.com/bitesize/articles/zx4ktv4
Learn more about why bees are attracted to flowers.

www.dkfindout.com/uk/animals-and-nature/insects/bee-colonies
Find out more about bee colonies.

Index